Space Voyager

Moon

by Vanessa Black

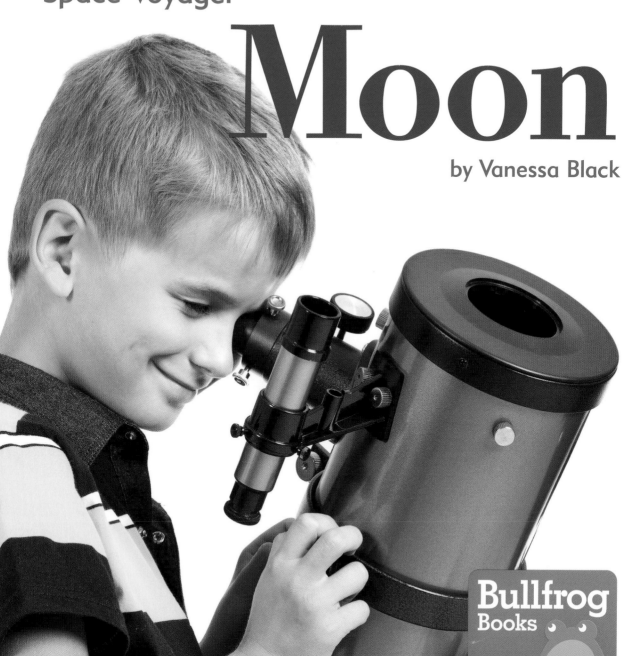

Bullfrog Books

Ideas for Parents and Teachers

Bullfrog Books let children practice reading informational text at the earliest reading levels. Repetition, familiar words, and photo labels support early readers.

Before Reading

- Discuss the cover photo. What does it tell them?

- Look at the picture glossary together. Read and discuss the words.

Read the Book

- "Walk" through the book and look at the photos. Let the child ask questions. Point out the photo labels.

- Read the book to the child, or have him or her read independently.

After Reading

- Prompt the child to think more. Ask: What are your favorite facts about the moon?

Bullfrog Books are published by Jump!
5357 Penn Avenue South
Minneapolis, MN 55419
www.jumplibrary.com

Library of Congress Cataloging-in-Publication Data

Names: Black, Vanessa, 1973– author.
Title: Moon / by Vanessa Black.
Description: Minneapolis, MN : Jump!, Inc., [2018]
Series: Space voyager
Audience: Age 5–8. | Audience: K to Grade 3.
Includes index.
Identifiers: LCCN 2017035427 (print)
LCCN 2017029943 (ebook)
ISBN 9781624966873 (ebook)
ISBN 9781620318461 (hardcover : alk. paper)
ISBN 9781620318478 (pbk.)
Subjects: LCSH: Moon—Juvenile literature.
Classification: LCC QB582 (print)
LCC QB582 .B585 2018 (ebook) | DDC 523.3—dc23
LC record available at https://lccn.loc.gov/2017035427

Editor: Jenna Trnka
Book Designer: Molly Ballanger
Photo Researchers: Molly Ballanger & Jenna Trnka

Photo Credits: NASA images/Shutterstock, cover; bloodua/iStock, 1; Delpixel/Shutterstock, 3; Bjarte Rettedal/Getty, 4; clintspencer/iStock, 5; Juergen Faelchle/Shutterstock, 6–7; klagyivik/iStock, 8–9; Danshutter/Shutterstock, 10–11, 23ml; Arvind Balaraman/Shutterstock, 12, 23tr; margo_black/Shutterstock, 13, 23br; Jessica Wilson/Science Source, 14–15; RomoloTravani/iStock, 16–17, 23tl; Castleski/Shutterstock, 18; NASA, 19; Blend Images - KidStock/Getty, 20–21 (boy); Yuganov Konstantin/Shutterstock, 20–21 (background); David Carillet/Shutterstock, 23mr; Business stock/Shutterstock, 23bl (hand); Tim UR/Shutterstock, 23bl (apple); iPhotoDesign/Shutterstock, 24.

Printed in the United States of America at Corporate Graphics in North Mankato, Minnesota.

Table of Contents

Earth's Moon

Look up!

What is that in the sky?

It is the moon.

It is the brightest thing in our night sky.

Why is it so bright?
It reflects the
sun's light.

The moon has phases.

It looks full.

This is when the sun shines fully on the moon.

full
moon

crescent
moon

Now it is a crescent.

Only part of it
is lit by the sun.

The moon orbits Earth.
It has its own gravity.

orbit

It pulls on the oceans.

It makes tides.

It is smaller than Earth.

It is made of rock.

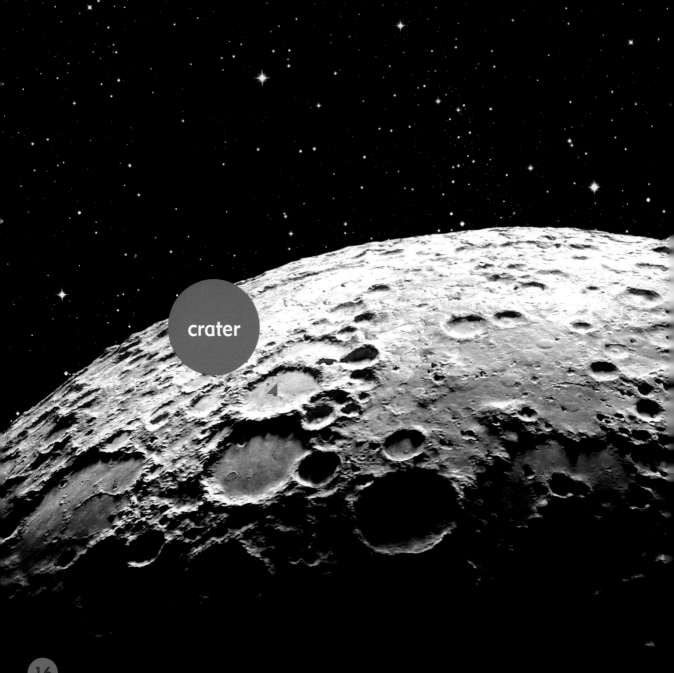

crater

The moon has craters.

Why?

Big rocks crashed into it.

We know a lot
about the moon.

How?

We have been there!

Someday we may go back.
Do you want to go?

A Look at the Moon

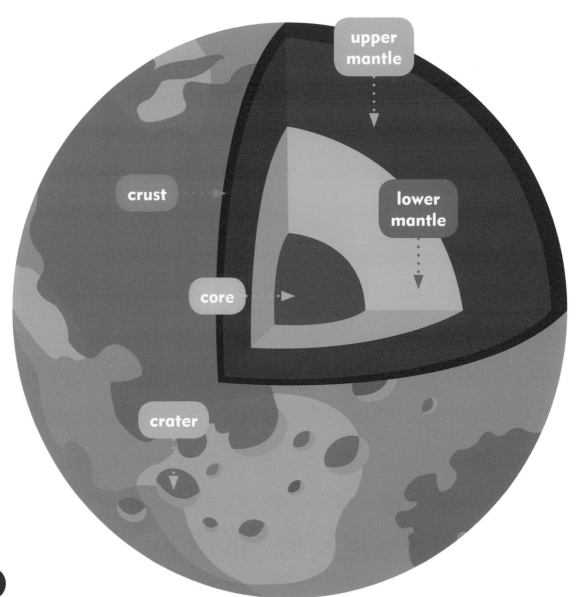

upper mantle

lower mantle

crust

core

crater

Picture Glossary

craters
Large round holes.

orbits
Travels around
in circles.

crescent
A phase of the
moon when less
than half of it is
lit up by the sun.

phases
The stages of the
moon's change in
shape as it appears
from Earth.

gravity
The force that
pulls things toward
the center of Earth
and keeps them
from floating away.

tides
The constant changes
in sea levels caused by
the pull of the sun and
the moon on Earth.

Index

To Learn More

Learning more is as easy as 1, 2, 3.

1) Go to www.factsurfer.com

2) Enter "moon" into the search box.

3) Click the "Surf" button to see a list of websites.

With factsurfer.com, finding more information is just a click away.